The
Single
Proverbs 31 Woman

A Guide to Being Beautiful Inside & Out

Alice Giraud

Verses marked KJV are taken from the King James Version of the Bible.

Verses marked NIV are taken from the HOLY BIBLE, NEW INTERNATIONAL VERSION. Copyright © 1973, 1978, 1984 by International Bible Society. Used by permission of Zondervan. All rights reserved.

Verses marked AMP are taken from AMPLIFIED BIBLE, Copyright © 1954, 1958, 1962, 1964, 1965, 1987 by The Lockman Foundation. All rights reserved. Used by permission. (www.Lockman.org)

Clip art © 2006 Jupiterimages Corporation

The Single Proverbs 31 Woman:
A Guide to Being Beautiful Inside & Out
ISBN 978-1-84728-802-8
Copyright © 2006 by Alice Giraud
AliceWrites.com

Printed in the United States of America. All rights reserved under International Copyright Law. Contents and/or cover may not be reproduced in whole or in part in any form without the express written consent of the Publisher or Author.

Dedications

The Strength of a Woman
<u>Carol & Lucille</u>
For teaching me how to remain strong in all circumstances and how to be the CEO of my household.

The Art of a Woman
<u>Marla, Alivia, DeAnnettia</u>
For showing me the other side of better living and the finer things in life. Your friendship is priceless.

The Essence of a Woman
<u>Michelle, Tiny, Cheryl, Etta, Kittoria, Leonard</u>
For your unconditional love, endless support and for keeping it real.

The Heart of a Woman
<u>Jose Giraud</u>
For giving me a heart for God since I was a little girl and for all of your sacrifice and hard work. Your tremendous love and affection has been my foundation for living a very fulfilled & happy life. I love you always.

Contents

Poem
7

Introduction
9

1 Who Can Find A Virtuous Woman?
13

2 She Can Be Trusted
19

3 She Is Willing To Work
25

4 She Is Domestic
33

5 She Plants & Cultivates
39

6 She Takes Care of Her Health & Body
45

7 She Is Confident
51

8 She Has A Generous Heart
57

9   She Protects Her Environment
63

10   She Dresses For Success & With Modesty
69

11   She Enhances Others
77

12   She is Business-Oriented
83

13   She Has Integrity
89

14   She Speaks with a Disciplined Tongue
95

15   She Occupies Her Time
101

16   She is Known by Her Fruit
105

17   She Strives for Excellence in All Things
111

18   She Surrenders Her Life to Christ
117

Who Can Find Her?

Who can find her?
The one that holds all attributes
She features qualities unattainable in others
Complete and full of substance
She's like the ocean
Filled with depth, always expanding
And reaching for more
Her intellect goes before her
Ask her about affairs in the Middle East,
Knowledge of the world feeds her
Ask her about commerce,
The business world excites her
You say… "Okay, she's smart,
But can she sew, cook and clean?"
And I say, she can do more.
Are you cold? She'll sew you a sweater
Are you hungry? She'll cook you a feast
Are you soiled? She'll make you spotless
She's socially balanced
She associates with all people
Rich, poor, bourgeoisie and urban
Those from the north, south and the suburban

If giving is the game,

Generosity is her name

She feeds the hungry and helps the disabled

You think this is it?

No, there's more…

She's physically fit,

Strong, energetic and fine

I know you're thinking,

"Wow, is she all that?"

And I say to you,

Yeah, fine as wine

With true beauty intertwined

But there's more…

Above all these things,

She serves the Lord.

Honorable and Godly

As she strives to please Him and live Holy

Who can find her?

- **Alice Giraud**

Introduction

Who can find a Proverbs 31 Woman? She is the hidden jewel that lives inside of every woman. Like a diamond in the rough, the Proverbs 31 Woman in you is waiting to be discovered to fulfill her God-given role and purpose. This highly esteemed woman in the scriptures represents all women at her highest dimension. God intended for all of us to embrace who we have been called to be, that is, women of excellence and virtue.

In Proverbs 31: 10-31, a description is given of what every woman, young and old, should strive to become. These scriptures depict a God-fearing woman at her core, which makes her who she is. Many readers of the Proverbs 31 Woman believe that no such woman exist and that it is impossible to meet these standards, particularly women of today. I beg to differ. What many overlook is that only her strengths are represented in Proverbs 31, not her weaknesses. In other words, the Proverbs 31 Woman is not mentioned as being perfect, but living in the maximized state that God created her to be in. This fulfillment makes her complete inside and out, in spite of her weaknesses. Even when we are at our absolute best, there will always be room for improvement as long as we live.

God does not expect us to be perfect, but He does expect us to always strive for perfection (Hebrews 13:21). In doing so, we should always purge ourselves of what hinders us to be at our best and at the same time, building ourselves up to be better than we were before.

Although this book focuses on the single woman, everyone can benefit from reading it. Men and women from all backgrounds, single, married, divorced or widowed, will be blessed by what God has to say about His precious daughters. Whether you are a single male interested to know what to look for in a future wife or a married woman looking to improve her character, this is the book for you. Whoever you are, as you read *The Single Proverbs 31 Woman: A Guide to Being Beautiful Inside & Out*, I pray that God speaks to your heart and move you to strive for excellence in every area of your life.

"Who can find a virtuous woman? For her price is far above rubies."

- Proverbs 31:10 KJV

1

Who Can Find A Virtuous Woman?

Who can find a virtuous woman? If you are a woman reading this book, take a second to look in the mirror and guess who you will see? Yes, the Proverbs 31 woman. For some of you it may be difficult to see this woman inside yourself because there are a lot of layers from your past and maybe even your present situation that need to be peeled away.

As a metal refiner that refines new found gold to eliminate all of its impurities and lackluster to reveal the true beauty of this fine metal for the world to see, so does God want to do the same in your life. Your past experiences, your failures and where you are today makes no difference. God has planted the seed of virtue inside every woman.

THE SINGLE PROVERBS 31 WOMAN

Perhaps you were or are still living a promiscuous lifestyle. Maybe you have lived your life on drugs or have been sexually abused. God wants to meet you right where you are and bring out His best in you. Remember that you are a creation of God and as the popular quote says, "God don't make no junk!" As a matter of fact, God loves to take what man thinks is impossible, shake it up a bit, put His glory on it and make the impossible possible. No matter what facet of life we are from, we all start out with God as diamonds in the rough. Some are rougher than others, but still a diamond, nonetheless. God recognizes our weaknesses, which makes us prime targets for God to come into our lives and begin a wonderful lifelong journey in walking with Him as the layers of our past hurts, mistakes and failures melt away.

No woman is born with all the strengths of this woman described in Proverbs. Many of us picked up traits and habits that are contrary to how God desires us to be from our environments as young children, authority figures in our lives and from popular social movements. The awesome thing about becoming who God has called you to be is that the attributes of the Proverbs 31 woman are learned. Some characteristics may come more naturally for some women and there are other attributes that will take a bit of work and that is okay. It is very important to point out that becoming a

Who Can Find A Virtuous Woman?

Proverbs 31 woman is not about becoming a cookie cut mold for all of us to look like identical robots that just stepped out the movie *The Stepford Wives*. We are not called to look alike, act alike or even feel the same way. We have been created with many different personalities with various gifts within us. Some of us are outspoken, some are shy and some are melancholy. I am someone that is very free-spirited and eclectic, yet there are some women that are more reserved and conservative. These personality traits are all gifts that we are to appreciate. We are all called to be different and God wants you to be you, but He wants you to be a better you, living in your maximized state.

"Her husband has full confidence in her and lacks nothing of value. She brings him good, not harm, all the days of her life."

- Proverbs 31:11-12 NIV

2

She Can Be Trusted

In this verse, the Bible refers to the husband trusting his Proverbs 31 wife, but since this book is geared towards single females, I will extract from this verse what is important for you to know in your unmarried state. As singles, instead of a spouse to care for, we are all responsible for caring for our families, friends and most importantly, the things of God. The time we spend cultivating all of our various relationships, trust is slowly built like a builder constructing a building, brick by brick.

Trust is the cornerstone of every relationship, but without it anything that was previously built will surely fall. If trust has been lost from the beginning of any relationship due to deceit and betrayal, it can be difficult to rebuild again.

THE SINGLE PROVERBS 31 WOMAN

Imagine someone in their backyard planting tomato seeds with the high anticipation of eating ripe, healthy, full-grown tomatoes. Although the soil was properly fertilized and good tomato seeds were planted, if the soil is suddenly devitalized, the seeds will not grow or if it does, the tomatoes will be discolored, the size will be retarded, the skin will be rough and you may even find worms and insects on the inside. Now, this is not to say that if trust has been lost in a relationship that it cannot be regained. Trust can always be earned again, but it is up to all parties involved if the relationship is worth rebuilding. If the relationship that has been destroyed due to trust involves a family member, they will be your relatives for life, but you can positively change the dynamics of the relationship with family members in such a way that you remain loving and courteous towards one another, depending on the circumstances of the betrayal of trust. You would have to judge the situation at your own discretion using God's wisdom.

Evaluate Your Heart

As a woman of God, you are called to be trustworthy. It is an essential characteristic to develop in relationships. You will never know who God will use to impact your life or help you to fulfill the calling on your life. If you cannot be trusted, then you limit what God can do for you. Even pertaining to the things of God, He has to be able to trust you in order for Him to promote you in your ministry, finances, career and in meeting your future spouse.

If you are wondering why you have not received a breakthrough in a certain area or if you think there is a lack of progression or promotion in your life, ask God to show you what you may be overlooking. Remember, God knows your heart, even if no one else does. To find out if you are someone others can trust, you must evaluate your heart and be honest with yourself. Do you have a tendency to use and manipulate others to get your way and what you want in life? Can you be trusted around the opposite sex, especially if that someone is already spoken for or married? Do you spread confidential information to those that should not know?
If you feel you need some work in becoming a trustworthy person, do not feel down on yourself. God already knows your weaknesses and although He already knows your heart,

THE SINGLE PROVERBS 31 WOMAN

He cannot intervene to help you until you come boldly to His throne of grace and ask for His help. Choose your own words, but with a sincere heart you can say something like this,

"God, I know I have messed up in the past, but I need your help. I ask for your forgiveness. Help me to be trustworthy, so I can have your best in every area of my life. Give me the wisdom I need to gain the trust of others. Thank you for your mercy and for your love. In Jesus name. Amen."

Our Father is faithful to forgive you and His compassion runs deep. He loves you no matter what mistakes you have made. God will always meet you at your point of need.

Trust is tied into your integrity, which I will go into detail about in a later chapter, but trust is essential for success in all of your relationships and in fulfilling God's calling on your life.

"She seeks out wool and flax and works with willing hands to develop it."

- Proverbs 31:13 AMP

3

She Is Willing To Work

As a single woman, working is a responsibility that most of us must carry out to meet our basic needs. We are finally waking up to the fact that work does not have to be a daunting task that fills our days just to pay bills. Many of us have jobs that we feel do nothing for us except provide a check so we can eat, have a roof over our head and for some, to take care of our families. Work should not only be a way to pay bills, but also to provide an opportunity to fuel our passions and a platform to exercise our talents and skills.

This verse in Proverbs 31:13 begins by saying, *"She seeks wool and flax..."* with an emphasis on the word *seeks*. During these times, women were skilled in making fine clothing by hand for their families and themselves using materials, such as wool and flax. Women also sold clothing as merchandise. Bringing this scripture up to modern times, not all women will know or even care to know how to actually make clothes by hand, but the point is that she was skilled or talented at something and she sought out how to put her skills to use. This brings me to my next point. If you feel that you don't have any skills or you have not discovered what your talents are, then you should first start with searching your heart to recognize what you enjoy doing and what you are passionate about.

There is a seed or some seeds that God has placed inside all of us. If you have not discovered what God has called you to do then your seeds may be lying dormant. First, let us find out exactly what talent, skills and abilities mean. The words *talent* and *skill* are often used interchangeably. According to the *American Heritage Dictionary*, talent is defined as a natural or acquired ability. In other words, your talent is either naturally endowed or it was acquired through some type of training. An example of a *natural endowment* is someone that can hear a song and begin to play it on an instrument without ever having to read or know how to read sheet music. Then there is *acquired talent* where some have to be trained in how to read music before they can ever play music on an instrument.

This *acquired talent* is also called *skill*. If it is a naturally endowed talent or an acquired skill, it is still talent and it is still a God-given talent.

Some people are bothered or jealous at those that are born with certain talents, but for some of us God wants us to be trained to acquire certain abilities to help make you the person He wants you to be. He may use your training to meet certain people that will help you along the way to fulfill your destiny or He will use your training to work on your character. The bottom line is that it is still talent and God will use whatever you have for His own purposes.

You Are Talented

Whether you know it or not, we all have been naturally endowed with a talent. You may have a gift of hospitality or the ability to work with children of a particular age. Some have a talent to lead or to manage a team of people. Ask God to help you in recognizing your natural gifts and if He is requiring you to get some training to enhance what you already have or to learn something new, don't complain about it. Do everything you can to bring out who you were meant to be.

THE SINGLE PROVERBS 31 WOMAN

God will only lead you to profit in every aspect of your life. *"…I am the Lord thy God which teacheth thee to profit, which leadeth thee by the way that thou shouldest go"* (Isaiah 48: 17 KJV).

Seek ways in how you can make the most of your talents. Be willing to do what it takes to be diligent in putting your hands to work. It is our responsibility before God to occupy our time and to create a platform for our gifts. Sometimes we ask God to bless us with new things or more abilities to fulfill our hearts desire, but if you are not being faithful with what you already have, you cannot expect Him to give you more. In the story of the three men with talents (Matthew 25:14-30), Jesus encouraged His disciples to use what they have to bear fruit, instead of sitting on what they have been given.

"Again, it will be like a man going on a journey, who called his servants and entrusted his property to them. To one he gave five talents of money, to another two talents, and to another one talent, each according to his ability. Then he went on his journey. The man who had received the five talents went at once and put his money to work and gained five more. So also, the one with the two talents gained two more. But the man who had received the one talent went off, dug a hole in the ground and hid his master's money.

She Is Willing To Work

After a long time the master of those servants returned and settled accounts with them. The man who had received the five talents brought the other five. 'Master,' he said, 'you entrusted me with five talents. See, I have gained five more!' His master replied, "Well done, good and faithful servant! You have been faithful with a few things; I will put you in charge of many things. Come and share your master's happiness!' The man with the two talents also came. 'Master,' he said, 'you entrusted me with two talents; see, I have gained two more.' Then the man who had received the one talent came. 'Master,' he said, 'I knew that you are a hard man, harvesting where you have not sown and gathering where you have not scattered seed. So I was afraid and went out and hid your talent in the ground. See, here is what belongs to you.' His master replied, 'You wicked, lazy servant! So you knew that I harvest where I have not sown and gather where I have not scattered seed? Well then, you should have put my money on deposit with the bankers, so that when I returned I would have received it back with interest. Take the talent from him and give it to the one who has the ten talents. For everyone who has will be given more and he will have an abundance. Whoever does not have, even what he has will be taken from him. And throw that worthless servant outside, into the darkness, where there will be weeping and gnashing of teeth."

THE SINGLE PROVERBS 31 WOMAN

Properly managing what God has given you is a commandment, not a suggestion. Give back to God what He has blessed you with by cultivating it and watch God multiply what you have given back to Him.

"She is like the merchant ships, bringing her food from afar. She gets up while it is still dark; she provides food for her family and portions for her servant girls."

- Proverbs 31:14-15 NIV

4

She Is Domestic

    As a young girl, I remember my mother, Lucille, always making my sister and I get in the kitchen and help her cut vegetables, mix ingredients and prepare dinner for the family. My sister and I would watch how our mother would put certain ingredients together to make delicious meals that everyone would love to eat. Even until this day, my other mom, Carol, and I will get in the kitchen together, so she can teach me how to cook her famous recipes that I still enjoy. Every time she is instructing me in how to prepare certain meals, she says, "You need to remember how to cook these meals to make dinner for yourself and for when you are married someday." These are some of the moments that I still benefit from as an adult. Although learning how to cook and clean were chores that I did not want to do because I just wanted to go outside and play or talk on the phone to my friends, I am so grateful for both of my mothers training me in household affairs.

A Woman's Work

Being domestic is the beginning to womanhood. Although many women of today's generation look down on being domestic, we are called to meet standards based on His word, not by the world's standards. The word domestic alone, has a negative connotation now because of how the world continues to confuse gender roles and pervert God's original design for man and woman. Domestic simply means to manage a household. Household management consist of keeping the home clean, being knowledgeable in creating meals, maintaining an atmosphere of peace and the list can go on and on. Being domestic is part of being a woman. God has designed us to nurture and care, not just for our loved ones, but also for the environment we reside in. As women, we have been blessed with the ability to add flair, comfort and the essentials for creating a paradise-like atmosphere. Yes, your home should be warm and loving and it should reflect who you are.

A few pieces of art on the wall, touched with a wonderful scent that fills the room, will do wonders in adding warmth to any room. There are many intricacies involved in keeping a home and it starts from where you are now as a single woman. What does your home look like right now? Are clothes all over the floor? Are dishes stacked up in the sink all of the time? Do you let just anyone into your place of dwelling? Open your mind to learning the details involved in managing your household because your home is a reflection of where your heart is and it is an extension of who you are.

The Woman

The final and most important aspect of being domestic is you, the woman. You can have a home that is absolutely beautiful, nothing out of place, with a sweet smell filling every room, but if you are unhappy, discontented and without peace, there is nothing in the world you can do to your home or for those in your home that will positively impact yourself and those that you are caring for. If you feel that you have not come to a place of peace and contentment in your life, it is never too late. God wants to fill your emptiness. If you find yourself always in search of something or someone to fill any holes in your heart, only God can give you what you are looking for.

THE SINGLE PROVERBS 31 WOMAN

If you are looking for peace, it is in Christ. If you are in need of direction and purpose, He will guide you. If you want to feel loved and wanted, God will fill your cup until it overflows. He will give you all you need to live a life of happiness and fulfillment. All you have to do is give Him your life. Hand over to Him all that is ailing you. Exchange your hurts and weaknesses for His strength, comfort and love. *"Casting all your care upon Him; for He careth for you"* (1 Peter 5:7 KJV).

"She considers a field and buys it; out of her earnings she plants a vineyard."

- Proverbs 31:16 AMP

5

She Plants & Cultivates

Imagine, a woman on her way to the movies and as she is driving, she just happens to look over and observes an empty two-story office building with a "For Sale" sign posted up on the front window. As she stops at a red light across the street from this land, she looks around the environment and right away recognizes that this would be a great area to start a consulting firm that she would often dream about owning someday. Long ago, she became frustrated at her 9 to 5 job that had ceased to fulfill her passion for counseling others in public relations because she longed for the freedom of working for herself someday. She drives on to the movie theatre, but she cannot get this idea of starting her own public relations firm in this building out of her mind.

THE SINGLE PROVERBS 31 WOMAN

After her movie, she decides to drive back to the property to write down the phone number on the sale sign to inquire about the price of the building. Right away, she calls, gets the price and more details about the property. This woman goes home to pray and ponder about this venture. After spending much time researching the start of her own business and hearing from God to go forth in this pursuit, she purchases the building and opens her long awaited public relations firm. After a few years of successfully running her firm that serves her local community, she begins to expand her existing business into an agency that serves companies around the country. Eventually, her public relations firm becomes highly sought after by Fortune 500 companies and is now listed on the Forbes list as one of the largest private companies.

There is a Dream in You

This story depicts a woman that planted and cultivated. Not every woman is called to start a business of her own, but the point is that we all have a seed inside of us that God expects us to plant and cultivate. What is your seed? You may have several seeds that are just waiting for you to work out in order to birth new ideas. Your dream may be to create a new department at your present job. Maybe you desire to start an on-line business. Your seed may be to become the CEO of your home, also known as a "stay at home mom," to nurture and care for your spouse and children. You may be called to be the Marketing Director at your job and sell your own line of jewelry on the side. There are no limits and no boundaries in God. He can inspire you with endless creative ideas. Allow yourself to step outside the box of what society considers the norm and God will take you places that you never thought possible. He wants us to gain new territory for Him, so stir up the gift that is in you (2 Timothy 1:6).

Once you have planted, your abilities have to be cultivated. Any seed that is planted, but not watered or cultivated will die or will grow with some kind of deformity. Whatever it is you do, you must tend to it for continued growth and expansion. For instance, if you are working for someone or a company, what can you do to improve your workplace? If your first response to that question is, "I'm doing just what I'm getting paid to do and nothing more," then you have already defeated yourself, your purpose and you have diminished any possibilities of any future opportunities. Anything you do that is over and beyond your work responsibilities is an investment in yourself, even if you are not getting paid for it. Never do just enough to get by or just enough to meet the status quo.

God expects us to excel in all things and if you are doing just enough to survive or just enough to keep a job, you have proven to God that He cannot trust you with a better position with more pay. Why would He promote you? Every season you are in and every job position you hold is an opportunity to prove to God that you can be trusted with more.

Begin to cultivate who you are and what you do. Increase your knowledge by learning something new. Read books in areas that can expand your thinking. Figure out ways in how you can improve your workplace. Make it a point to change the atmosphere wherever you are by always being positive and encouraging others. When you plant and cultivate what you have, you give God the chance to bless you in greater ways that you never thought possible.

"She girdeth her loins with strength and strengtheneth her arms."

- Proverbs 31:17 KJV

6

She Takes Care of Her Health & Body

I think you can never talk too much about improving ones health. Although there is so much information available on eating right and exercise, we still have a long way to go. According to the American Heart Association, heart disease is the number one killer of women in America with cancer being a close second. Our health has to become a priority for us because if we are always in pain and always out of breath, we deny ourselves the opportunity to enjoy life as we should and to be a blessing to others. If you are already on the road to good health through daily exercise and eating healthy food, then I commend you. In this chapter, I want to focus more on the importance of a woman fulfilling her responsibility of taking care of her own body.

THE SINGLE PROVERBS 31 WOMAN

Sometimes we get so caught up in caring for others that we forget about ourselves, but if we don't care for ourselves, who will? You certainly don't want the doctors or loved ones to have to bear the burden of caring for you if you are bedridden or if you are immobile due to an illness that could have been prevented through living a healthy lifestyle. Do not feel guilty about making yourself a priority in caring for your health because you will not be any good to your family and in what God has called you to do if you are sick all of the time.

Some of us are in our 30's and 40's and still have not met our future spouse and have not had children yet. This really motivates me to stay in shape, so when I do marry and have children, I will still have stamina, vigor and good health to be at my very best in caring for my family. If you feel that you have a long way to go in meeting your goals in your pursuit to achieving a healthy body, don't feel discouraged. You may want to just lose the extra 10 pounds you have been fighting for the past year or maybe you want to lose 80 pounds to feel better. Some of you may be happy where you are, but you would like to feel more energetic during the day.

No matter how old you are or how busy you are, it is never too late. Once you know what your goals are, it is important to meet with a fitness expert that can inform you on how you can meet your goals. Even if you cannot afford

She Takes Care of Her Health & Body

to pay for a fitness expert, you can always learn how to eat healthy by going on the internet or purchasing a book on healthy living. Exercising can be done in your home with the purchase of fitness videos or you can join a gym if that works better for you. With so much free education and information available on the internet today, there is no reason why you cannot learn how to begin making the changes needed in your life. Yes, it takes work and diligence, but it is worth the effort and time.

Making lifestyle changes is up to you and no one is going to do it for you. God has given us the responsibility to take care of our bodies. We are to glorify Him with our precious vessels through proper nutrition and exercise.

I know by experience that battling with our favorite foods and dealing with gluttony is not an easy feat to conquer. I have fought the battle of the bulge for many years, until God showed me that if I stop depending on my own strength, renew my mind with His word and allow the power of the Holy Spirit to comfort me during the stormy times, my lust for food could be overcome. If you have also fought this weakness for a long time, please do not give up, your life depends on it. Seek God's ways and saturate yourself with His word to help change your thinking about food.

THE SINGLE PROVERBS 31 WOMAN

Also, educate yourself on what are healthy foods and implement some type of exercise program into your daily schedule.

To successfully conquer this issue, you must take the spiritual and the natural into account and apply them to your life on a daily basis, until it is no longer a struggle for you. God will help you every step of the way.

"She perceiveth that her merchandise is good, her candle goeth not out by night. She layeth her hands to the spindle and her hands hold the distaff."

- Proverbs 31:18-19 KJV

7

She Is Confident

Ladies, confidence looks good on you! Anywhere you go, your chin should be up, shoulders back and swaying as if you are modeling on your own runway. Know that you are beautiful because you are a special creation of God. No matter what your size is, only women have curves and dips that were purposely created to differentiate us from men and to tantalize the eyes of our husbands.

We should also feel confident about our performance in our career, ministry, caring for our families and anything else we put our hands to. Feeling good about yourself begins with knowing who you are in Christ. We all have flaws, weaknesses and things to improve upon, but understand first and foremost that, in spite of it all, you are still complete in Him. God loves you, in spite of your failures, mistakes and imperfections.

THE SINGLE PROVERBS 31 WOMAN

For I am convinced that neither death nor life, neither angels nor demons, neither the present nor the future, nor any powers, neither height nor depth, nor anything else in all creation, will be able to separate us from the love of God that is in Christ Jesus our Lord" (Romans 8:38-39).

If you feel that you lack confidence in general, begin to read and meditate on God's Word. I have listed a few scriptures that you can get started with to sow into your heart on a daily basis.

Scriptures on Confidence

Proverbs 3:26
Romans 5:5
Ephesians 3:11-12
1 John 3:18-24
1 John 4:4

Feeling confident in how well you perform in certain areas in your life can be attained. For example, if you feel uncomfortable speaking in front of a group of people, you can improve by taking public speaking classes to learn techniques in getting over stage fright and speaking without fumbling over your words and anything else you may need help with. If you enjoy playing tennis, but you are not confident enough to play in a tournament, take tennis lessons

She Is Confident

to improve your game. The more you practice, the better you get, the more confidence you will gain.

When you are confident, it shows in your walk, your stance, your conversation and in the things you do. Confidence exudes from the inside out and it reveals that you know who you are. Confidence gives you self-assurance and it gives you an appeal to others that makes them want to know you better. This creates great opportunities for new friendships and for blessing people's lives.

"She opens her arms to the poor and extends her hands to the needy."

- Proverbs 31:20 NIV

8

She Has A Generous Heart

A generous heart means that you are a cheerful giver and you are always looking for ways to be a blessing to others. We are required by God to be good stewards over all that we have been blessed with and to be economically sound in the handling of our finances. Good stewardship over what God has given us is an attribute that everyone should work towards.

No matter what financial state you are in, God has called all of us to be givers. Hoarding anything that you have is unattractive and more importantly, you rob yourself the opportunity to be blessed with more. *"Give and [gifts] will be given to you; good measure, pressed down, shaken together, and running over, will they pour into [pour formed by] the bosom [of your robe and used as a bag].*

THE SINGLE PROVERBS 31 WOMAN

For with the measure you deal out [with the measure you use when you confer benefits on others], it will be measured back to you" (Luke 6:38 AMP). There are many areas that we can give ourselves to and our finances.

We are to help those that are in need and in unfortunate circumstances. We should also give generously for the spreading of the gospel around the world, so all people can have the opportunity to learn about Christ and live better lives (Mark 16:15). Generosity is not just about money, it also includes the giving of self and your time. When we are so consumed with our own problems and issues our hearts are feeling heavy and down, but you will be surprised that if we step outside of ourselves to help another during our darkest times, joy begins to enter your heart because you are thinking of someone else. You may even realize that your situation is not as bad as it seems.

Those of us that have made Jesus Christ our Lord and Savior should be known for our generosity. Giving reflects the love of Christ and who we are in Him. Some of you may feel that you have nothing to give, but there is always something you have that can bless someone's life. Look around your home. Maybe you have a new dress that has been sitting in your closet for the past year or a pair of shoes that you have never worn. You always have something to give. Don't discount what you have because someone else may consider it a real treasure.

"When it snows, she has no fear for her household; for all of them are clothed in scarlet."

- Proverbs 31:21 NIV

9

She Protects Her Environment

The Proverbs 31 woman prays for protection over her home, her family and herself. She is confident that God has given His angels charge over her and all that she has declared, so her sleep is sweet and peace resides in her and in her home.

Your environment consist of your surroundings including your home, the company you consistently keep and anywhere you spend most of your time. I always say, "You are what your environment is." You may have also heard people say, "If you want to know what your future will be like, look at the company you keep." You will only rise as high as those you spend most of your time with. Who you associate with is very crucial to your success in your personal life, your spiritual life, your finances and in your career. Evaluate any relationships and activities that you are currently involved in and consider who and what may be a hindrance to you having God's best in your life. Do you have any friendships that are toxic? Are you in a relationship of the opposite sex that encourages and pressures you to live an ungodly lifestyle? If so, you must decide for yourself if you are going to settle for what the world has to offer or if you are willing to pursue God's best for your life. Conducting your life as the world does will only bring misery, pain and regret. Yes, you will have fun for awhile and yes, you may get what you want for awhile, but it is very temporary and you will always get the short end of the stick. Your Creator knows what is best for you and if He is telling you to let certain relationships go or to stop going certain places, it is only because He is trying to get you into His place of blessings. God will not bless you with the husband you have always dreamed of having if you continue to stay with someone that you know you have no business being with in the first place.

    Surrender to your Father in heaven because He has a plan for your life. As long as you are doing your own thing and living your own way, then God is not obligated to direct you into what He has for you. Give your life over to Him and you will begin to see God moving on your behalf.

She Protects Her Environment

If you surrender your love life, your finances, your career and every area of your life, you give Him the opportunity to enter your life to show you His plan for your life.

What God has is better than what the world has to offer, but you will never know if you don't surrender. Jesus loves you and He is waiting for you with open arms.

"She makes coverings for her bed; she is clothed in fine linen and purple."

- Proverbs 31:22 NIV

10

She Dresses For Success & With Modesty

In biblical times, queens and women in high positions would send for linens and silk from Egypt and India. She would also send for purple cloth from the Phoenician emporium to make fine clothing for herself. It was important for women that held important positions to represent themselves, their families and the kingdoms they belonged to by always looking their absolute best.

Wherever you are in life, you are a queen in your own right and the way you dress should say so without you ever having to say a word. Not every one is in a financial position to wear the latest fashion designer clothing, but you can always make the best out of what you have available. Starting with the very basics is maintaining a neat and clean appearance. Looking well-groomed by keeping your hair together at all times and wearing clothes that fit you well, never too tight, but clothing that bring out the best in you no matter what your size is. I know for some of us that work out in the gym or are involved in outdoor recreational activities, looking neat is not exactly the goal because you need to wear comfortable clothes and remain focused on your workouts, but you should always do at least the minimum. You don't have to look like a superstar in the gym, after all, no one looks like a star when you are concentrating on sweating, lifting and burning calories.

Invest in some decent workout clothes that look good on you, but are comfortable to exercise in. Put your hair up in a ponytail or pin it up, so your crown is looking good after sweating it out in the gym. Do what works best for you, but still maintain a decent appearance. You will never know who you may run into at anytime.

You Are Called To A Higher Standard

Today is the era of "baring it all," but modesty will beat showing all of your goods every time. You may get a few looks and some attention, but ultimately you will be treated the way you are dressed. You can ask most men and they will say the same thing. No one respects a woman that is

She Dresses For Success & With Modesty

trying to gain attention from baring it all, although some wandering eyes are upon her. It is always obvious to everyone else, but the woman showing all her goods is, usually, oblivious to the fact that she is showing a lack of respect for herself. Dressing modestly does not mean that you have to walk around with long skirts down to your ankle and blouses buttoned to the very top of your neck. It means to use sound judgment in what you wear and be considerate about who you are around.

Unfortunately, lack of judgment in this area is even creeping into churches. You can look just as beautiful wearing a skirt at a modest length, than wearing one that will reveal all of your glory if you make the slightest movement. If you feel good about yourself and you are dressed with class and modesty, you will be surprised about the positive attention you will receive. We are all queens in the sight of God and the way we dress should befit a queen.

THE SINGLE PROVERBS 31 WOMAN

Dress for Success

Dressing for success means to dress for opportunities that you are believing God for and dressing the part for the different roles of your career, ministry and any other areas that require you to look a particular way. If you are in faith for a lead position in your church, make sure you are dressed for the part. If you desire to become an executive in your office, then you should dress like one. What you wear speaks for you before you have a chance to say anything about yourself. What do you want your clothes to say about you? If you want respect, you should dress in a respectable manner. If you want to be successful in your line of work, your look should say so.

How you look speaks a thousand words. If you think you have some areas you need to work on, learn to make the most out of what you have. If you are not sure what looks good on you, then ask a close friend that you trust to give you some pointers. It really helps to have someone else look us over and offer some suggestions if it is needed. Sometimes outsiders can see what the mirror does not tell us.

She Dresses For Success & With Modesty

Remember, before you dress, always think about what kind of message you want to send to others. You will never know who you may meet and what opportunities may present themselves at any given moment.

"Her husband is respected at the city gate, where he takes his seat among the elders of the land."

- Proverbs 31:23 NIV

11

She Enhances Others

Verse 23 describes the Proverbs 31 woman's husband as being well-known among his peers and highly respected by those in authority of the land. The purpose of this passage is to make it known that her husband is highly looked upon by his peers and his colleagues because his wife is an enhancement to him. She encourages him often in his affairs outside of the home. His wife takes care of the household, so he will have nothing to worry about and he is able to focus on providing for the family. She helps him in his weaknesses and she brings value to his character. This virtuous woman is profitable for her husband and everyone in the land knows that he is a great man because his wife brings out the best in him. As single women, we can learn a lot from this passage. In our singleness, we should be a blessing to our friends, families and others that cross our path. God has raised you up to positively change the atmosphere wherever you go. Enhancing others means to be a light when others see nothing but darkness. As a result, you help those around you to see the best in themselves and in their own circumstances. It does not mean that you will be able to help everyone, but by having a positive attitude and an encouraging word, you can make a difference in someone else's life.

Sometimes just by living a Godly lifestyle and a healthy outlook on life can inspire others to change their perspective on how they view life. God will use anything you have to get someone's attention in order to redirect their path.

You will not always know when God is using you. Many times I have been blessed by just watching others live a flourishing lifestyle due to their obedience to God. Just simply observing great men and women of God inspires me and reminds me that if I am obedient to the things of God, He will see to it that my needs are met and that I have the desires of my heart. Think about the times when just one word from an entire conversation or a sermon changed your life. You, too, can do the same for others.

She Enhances Others

Live and know that God can use your words and your lifestyle to change someone's heart and life. Be mindful of the things you do and say because God just might be waiting to use you to enhance another person's life.

"She makes linen garments and sells them, and supplies the merchants with sashes."

- Proverbs 31:24 KJV

12

She Is Business-Oriented

Linen was considered a very high quality fabric that women of the bible used to make and sell clothing. This passage, along with verse 14 and 18 tells that this woman knew how to make money. The Proverbs 31 woman uses whatever skills she has for commerce.

All women should be business-oriented on some level. Every woman is not destined to start a business, but she should have something under her belt that she can use to bring in some money if she desires or if it is needed to help meet your needs. The skill or that thing you may need to stir up the business side of you may be getting a degree of your interest or learning something new. You can use something you enjoy doing like arts and crafts. It can be a small passion or a hobby that you relish that maybe you could turn into a side business for profit. But if you get joy just from making it a hobby only and not for profit, that is great too. As long as you have something that could be used for something greater if needed.

Catching up on current affairs and the business world through reading books, magazines and newspapers is another way to become business-oriented. You can learn about business deals, the economy and the marketplace. This can improve the social aspect of your life because you can always join others in conversations that are discussing the latest in news and matters of the world. Also, it can increase your intellect, knowledge and your self-confidence.

Don't let your occupation or background dictate what you should learn. Realize that educating yourself on a new subject, especially if it is not related to what you do for a living, just might elevate your thinking and improve your perspective on life. As a result, your new knowledge could end up taking you places you have never been.

The business world may seem a little intimidating, but once you expose yourself to it, you will see that it is not as scary as it may seem.

At the very minimum, I would suggest reading business magazines, such as *Fortune, Black Enterprise* and *Forbes*. I highly recommend reading *The Wall Street Journal,* even if

She is Business-Oriented

you feel that you are clueless about world and business events. The *WSJ* is loaded with information that can enlarge your view of the world and educate you on some of the basics of business. It is an easy way to get started and to inform yourself about financial markets, politics and world affairs.

Business matters have a great impact on all of our lives directly or indirectly, so it is important to teach yourself about what makes the world go around.

"Strength and honor are her clothing and she shall rejoice in time to come."

- Proverbs 31:25 KJV

13

She Has Integrity

The way you set yourself apart from others is to be a woman of integrity. Everyone knows how you are in front of people and in the public, but who really are you behind closed doors? Integrity is who you are when no one is looking. You may be commended often at the workplace about how great of a job you are doing, but when no one is looking, are you taking pens, paper clips and staplers home? When you are in church, you are smiling at everyone and saying, "Praise the Lord," to your fellow church members, but when you get in the car and someone cuts you off in traffic, how do you respond? See, this is where the rubber meets the road. God is not impressed with trickery, manipulation and false character. You may be fooling people, but you can never fool God Almighty. In Jeremiah 17:10, God says, *"I the Lord search the heart, I try the reins, even to give every man according to his ways and according to the fruit of his doings."*

He will never promote someone and send them to the next level if there is a lack of integrity, until He sees that you can be trusted in *every* area of your life. Perhaps you feel that you can be trusted in only one area of your life and that should cover it all. You may be someone that your friends and family can depend on financially, but can you be trusted around someone's boyfriend or husband? Do you manipulate and use people to get what you want? I ask these hard questions because if you don't conquer this area first, then having all the money, looks and friends in the world means nothing.

In Proverbs 11:3 it says that *"The integrity of the upright shall guide them...,"* and if you are not a person of integrity, you cannot expect God to lead you to His place of blessings and abundance. However, God will honor you if you find that you need help in this area of your life and you want to change to become the true woman He has intended you to be. You may not know how to change because this is the only way you know how to get by in life. Give your Heavenly Father the opportunity to come into your life and change your heart. He loves you and He wants to bless you abundantly and give you all He has waiting for you, but you have to be willing to relinquish everything you have and everything you are to God. That includes your heart, your mind and your soul. You have nothing to lose and everything to gain. If you have wondered why things haven't been working out for you, no matter how hard you have tried, search your heart and evaluate your life. Be honest with yourself and with God because remember, He already knows. He is just waiting on you to come to Him. It does not matter how much of a mess you think you are, the blood of Jesus runs deep. He loves you wherever you are in life. Ask Him to forgive you and God will embrace you. He is always faithful to forgive.

"If we confess our sins, he is faithful and just to forgive us our sins, and to cleanse us from all unrighteousness."

- 1 John 1:9 KJV

"She speaks with wisdom, and faithful instruction is on her tongue."

- Proverbs 31:26 NIV

14

She Speaks With A Disciplined Tongue

Don't you wish we could just say whatever we want to say and whenever we want to say it? Many of us would be in lots of trouble if we did. Some people do anyway, but words said the wrong way or at the wrong time will always bite you in the end, even if you don't realize it. Speaking with a disciplined tongue takes work, especially for those that love to talk.

There is a time to speak and a time to stay silent, just as there is a time to laugh and a time to cry. It can be a challenge sometimes to know when it is necessary to interject in order to give words of wisdom or to let God deal with a particular person. Even in casual conversation with friends, it is easy to speak out of turn and to say more than is necessary or give too much information. And if you are not aware that you are saying something that should not be said, you are usually the last to know or most times everyone else knows, except you. I think we are all guilty of putting our foot in our mouth at one time or another, some a lot more than others.

Think Before You Speak

To start, it is important to remain conscious of what words you use, how you say it and when you say it. This includes times when you are in a professional setting, formal setting and casual setting. This is worth putting forth an effort to work on because what you say exposes who you really are, even if you are trying to conceal a matter with your words.

"...For out of the overflow of the heart the mouth speaks."

- Matthew 12:34 NIV

Speak With Wisdom & Kindness

The rule of thumb to follow is to "think before you speak." Assess the situation, the conversation and the people involved. Consider if what you want to say is something that should be said. Don't put yourself in bondage feeling that you have to walk on egg shells every time you are holding a conversation. Just be careful and considerate when you speak. Your words reflect your character, your heart and most of all, the God you serve. *"...In her tongue is the law of kindness"* (Proverbs. 31: 26 KJV). What is in your tongue? Words that come out of our mouth should be of wisdom, encouragement and kindness. That also includes times when you don't feel like being kind. It is easy to say nice things when others are nice to us, but the true test of who you really are is when the pressure is on. There will always be times when we are in situations when we have to deal with people that have bad attitudes and that have a negative disposition. These are great opportunities to practice disciplining your tongue. Just because some one gets irate with you does not mean you have to respond in the same manner. Keep a cool head by taking a deep breath and remember you are a child of God.

THE SINGLE PROVERBS 31 WOMAN

Be firm, if necessary, but speak in a controlled, normal tone of voice and be careful in choosing your words.

"A soft answer turneth away wrath: but grievous words stir up anger."
-Proverbs 15:1 KJV

You can speak with wisdom and intelligence and still get your point across. There are some battles that you have to learn to walk away from, instead of going back and forth on who is right or who is wrong. Ask God to give you wisdom in this area and He will teach you along the way (James 1:5). Remember, your words are who you are, so be mindful in conversation and in your daily interactions with others.

"She watches over the affairs of her household and does not eat the bread of idleness."

- Proverbs 31:27 NIV

15

She Occupies Her Time

If you feel as if you don't have a life, the best way to get one is by getting a hobby. That may not sound exciting because when many people think of the word hobby, they tend to think of doing something that bores them. A hobby is a passion that you may have for a particular activity. You've got to get creative. Hobbies can be anything you enjoy doing during your spare time. Dancing, playing an instrument, reading, working out or taking a class to learn something new are all examples of a hobby. Do something to occupy your time that brings you joy and expands your mind and your spirit. It should be something that is constructive. If you don't have a hobby, you will be surprised as to how much it fulfills you and helps you to feel better about yourself.

THE SINGLE PROVERBS 31 WOMAN

When you are idle all of the time, we tend to get ourselves in trouble one way or another. If you are just sitting around with nothing constructive to do, you can be tempted to call up people to entertain you that you know are nothing but trouble. We eat more food to help fill that time of idleness, gaining unwanted pounds. You may even begin to consume yourself with negative thoughts about your situation or family life, which can easily fester into depression and anxiety. Occupying your time is crucial to feeling better about your life and experiencing more of what God has to offer. There is a very big world out there with countless things to do and to learn about, so why deny yourself the opportunity of having more in your life and improving your mind, your body and your spirit. So, get out there and purposely search for a hobby or find your passion. You will never regret feeling good and looking well because you are occupying your time doing something that is fulfilling, healthy and fun.

"Her children arise and call her blessed; her husband also, and he praises her."
"Give her the reward she has earned, and let her works bring her praise at the city gate."

- Proverbs 31:28 & 31 NIV

16

She Is Known By Her Fruit

When you walk by a tree, you can tell what kind of a tree it is by the fruit it yields. If you see apples hanging from its branches, it is an apple tree. Your fruit is the result of the way you live, whether it is good fruit or bad fruit. It comes out in your daily attitude towards others and life. Your fruit is seen in how you interact with others. Are you always starting arguments or do you bring peace to any atmosphere?

The fruit you produce is reflected in what you do for other people. Being a blessing to those that cross your path is good fruit. Cursing someone out because they got your order wrong at a restaurant is bad fruit. What you give unto the Kingdom and what you do for those in need is good fruit. Hoarding everything you receive is rotten fruit.

THE SINGLE PROVERBS 31 WOMAN

"Make a tree good and its fruit will be good, or make a tree bad and its fruit will be bad, for a tree is recognized by its fruit."

-Matthew 12:33 NIV

What You Sow is What You Reap

Your fruit is a reflection of your heart. Seeds that you sow into your heart are what come out as fruit.

"Be not deceived; God is not mocked: for whatsoever a man soweth, that shall he also reap."

-Galatians 6:7 KJV

Everyday seeds are being sown into your life through what you hear, what you see and what you say. If you are always around people that are complaining and are discontent with their life, eventually you will be the same way. Listening to sad, "My baby left me" music all of the time will cause you to feel sad and depressed. Be careful in what you expose yourself to, it could determine the way you live and how you affect others. Negativity is contagious.

Seek God to find out what He has purposed you to do in the world. Allow Him to work with you and expand your heart for Him and His works. Only then will you be in a position to bear good fruit and bear lots of it. Bearing fruit is another way of saying that you are using everything God has given you to be productive, effective, changing people's lives for the better and to advance the Kingdom of God. When you do this, God will bless you abundantly in every area of your life, so that you can be even more fruitful in the earth. The parable of the talents that Jesus told to his disciples explains this principle of sowing and reaping. Sowing into others and into the Kingdom of God will cause you to reap the benefits of what you have given. If you give, more will be given back to you abundantly.

"...Well done, thou good and faithful servant: thou hast been faithful over a few things, I will make thee ruler over many things: enter thou into the joy of thy lord."

-Matthew 25:21 KJV

When you are fruitful, your work will speak for itself. God will honor what you have done. After blessing others, never look for appreciation or a thank you from people, although it is always nice to hear, but expect your reward from God, not man. Even if men do not recognize what you have given or done, continue to keep a smile on your face in knowing that God is always looking and He will honor you in what you have done.

THE SINGLE PROVERBS 31 WOMAN

"Therefore, my beloved brethren, be firm (steadfast), immovable, always abounding in the work of the Lord [always being superior, excelling, doing more than enough in the service of the Lord], knowing and being continually aware that your labor in the Lord is not futile [it is never wasted or to no purpose]."

-1 Corinthians 15:58 AMP

"Many daughters have done virtuously, nobly, and well [with the strength of character that is steadfast in goodness], but you excel them all."

-Proverbs 31:29 KJV

17

She Strives For Excellence In All Things

Excellence is a small detail that makes the most profound impact in differentiating someone or something from being better to the best, from average to superior. It is a quality that can separate you from the rest of the pack. Excellence requires going the extra mile, whether it is pursuing excellence at the workplace, how you look or making a presentation to a group of people.

Many disregard the attribute of excellence because it does take extra effort and we all have our moments when we really don't feel like going over and above. Achieving excellence does not mean that you are perfect and that you never make mistakes. You can be imperfect and still be excellent. It means that you exhaust every resource you have and honestly doing your very best in everything you put your hands to. After you have done all you can do, God steps in and takes care of the rest.

Your goal in pursuing excellence should be to never settle for mediocrity. Mediocrity causes complacency, which will always guarantee that you will end up with second best in everything. It may cause a little initial pain to do the extra work it takes to excel, but in the end you will be happy you did.

During most of my years in school, I had only done enough work to get by. I just did not feel like doing what it required to get A's & B's, although I knew I could have if I would have done the extra studying and preparation. When I got to college, after one semester, I realized I could not pull the same stunts I did when I was younger in order to get by. I had to either do everything it took to excel in my studies or I would not graduate. I made the decision to improve my time management by putting myself on a daily study schedule and I hired tutors to help me in classes that I struggled in, which was something I would have never done in the past. I did not have any money to pay tutors on a weekly basis, but I was so determined to exhaust all of my resources. I braided hair on the side and worked an on-campus job to pay for tutoring.

She Strives For Excellence In All Things

It took a lot of my time and sleep, but God honored it because He knew I gave everything I had to graduate. In the end I graduated without any problems.

Ultimately, you are giving God your best when you strive for excellence in every aspect of life. Never settle for less. Do your best in everything, otherwise you have defeated yourself and nullified God's plan for your life. You are a precious gift of God and only the best will do!

"Charm and grace are deceptive, and beauty is vain [because it is not lasting], but a woman who reverently and worshipfully fears the Lord, she shall be praised!"

- Proverbs 31:31 KJV

18

She Surrenders Her Life To Christ

In all of our efforts to be beautiful inside and out, nothing stands out more than a woman that has handed her life over to the One that made the ultimate sacrifice for us by giving His life, Jesus Christ. Looking good on the outside, along with having a beautiful heart makes a big difference in our lives, but it all means nothing if Christ is not the center of your life. He can turn your life into a rose that is in full bloom, if only you let Him.

If you think you are happy where you are now in your own life, then God can make it even better. If things have not gone your way and you find yourself always struggling to find peace, joy and happiness, you will find it in your Heavenly Father. Even if you consider yourself to be the most beautiful woman in the world, physical beauty will never bring the fulfillment that many search for in other people, money and things. God will meet you right where you are. Don't try to clean your life up and then come to God because you cannot clean your life up on your own. Nothing else has worked. Give God an opportunity to help you become the woman you have always desired to be.

Exchange your weaknesses for His strength and He will give you beauty for ashes. Real and true beauty is what He gives to help you flourish in your life beyond what you have ever dreamed.

"To appoint unto them that mourn in Zion, to give unto them beauty for ashes, the oil of joy for mourning, the garment of praise for the spirit of heaviness; that they might be called trees of righteousness, the planting of the Lord, that He might be glorified."
-Isaiah 61:3 KJV

Become Who You Really Are

All women are called to be the Proverbs 31 woman. Yes, even you. Let God peel off the layers that have kept you from being your best. We have all experienced situations that leave battle scars causing us to be tired, frustrated and wanting to give up on life. God Almighty knows you and He knows all that you have been through. He knew you before you were even born (Jeremiah 1:5). He is saying to you today to surrender your love life, your finances, your career and everything else to Him.

Trust Him to turn things around for you. It does not mean that you still won't have challenges, but the difference is that you will have peace in the midst of it all. When the storms of life feel like they are crashing down, God will empower you to be unmovable and victorious in every situation that comes your way.

If you have not accepted Jesus Christ as your Lord and Savior, with a sincere heart, read the following prayer for salvation. Salvation is a gift that you receive by just saying that you believe in Him and you accept Him into your life. It does not matter how much wrong you have done or how many mistakes you feel you have made.

THE SINGLE PROVERBS 31 WOMAN

Accept Christ into your heart and He will abide with you from this day forward to show you who He is and to reveal the beautiful person you are through Him.

Prayer for Salvation

"Father, I believe that Jesus died on the cross for me. I believe you raised Jesus from the dead, so that I may live. I accept you Jesus Christ as my Lord and Savior. Forgive me for my sins. Thank you for washing my sins away with your blood. I surrender my life to you from this day forward. Fill me with your Holy Spirit. Heavenly Father, I am your child. Show me your way and show me how to live for you. Thank you for your saving grace and for loving me. In Jesus name. Amen."

Books by Alice Giraud Coming Soon…

Patiently Waiting for the One

To correspond with Alice Giraud,

E-mail her at books@alicewrites.com

Or log on to her website at:

www.AliceWrites.com